DATE DUE

PRINTED IN U.S.A.

VOLLEYBALL
GIRLS ROCKING IT

KAT MILLER and CLAUDIA B. MANLEY

ROSEN
PUBLISHING

NEW YORK

Published in 2016 by The Rosen Publishing Group, Inc.
29 East 21st Street, New York, NY 10010

First Edition

Library of Congress Cataloging-in-Publication Data

Miller, Kat.
 Volleyball : girls rocking it / Kat Miller and Claudia B. Manley. — First Edition.
     pages cm. — ((Title IX Rocks! Play Like a Girl))
 Includes index.
 ISBN 978-1-5081-7045-7 (Library bound)
 1. Volleyball for girls—Juvenile literature. I. Manley, Claudia B. II. Title.
 GV1015.4.W66M55 2016
 796.325082—dc23

                                                    2015018393

Manufactured in China

CONTENTS

INTRODUCTION

Have you ever played volleyball or watched a volleyball game? Volleyball is a fast-paced sport and it is easy to get caught up in the excitement of the game. While the most commonly played kind of volleyball is indoor volleyball, beach volleyball is also very popular. Both versions of the game require players to develop a range of athletic skills and work well with teammates.

While there are also professional volleyball players, the sport is most widely played in schools. It makes frequent appearances in gym classes across the United States and Canada. It's also a popular competitive sport. Teams compete in multiple divisions at both the high school and the college level.

While both men and women—and girls and boys—play volleyball, it's actually a female-dominated sport at the competitive level. There are roughly eight female volleyball players for every male player at the high-school level and about eleven female players for every male player at the college level.

There are around 430,000 high school women's volleyball players, according to the National Federation of State High School Associations' High School Athletics Participation Survey. According to the National Collegiate Athletic Association (NCAA), there are more than twenty-six thousand women who play at the college level. There are lots of opportunities to play at the high school and college

Thousands of talented female athletes play volleyball. Here, players from Briar Woods High School and Princess Anne High School compete in the Virginia 5A State Volleyball Championship.

level in Canada, too. Ontario alone has more then thirty universities with volleyball teams.

The number of women involved in volleyball has grown steadily over the past few decades. One of the factors that has allowed this to happen was the passing of Title IX in 1972. Title IX is a section of the Education Amendments of 1972, a US law. Title IX requires that schools that receive federal funding need to provide equal opportunities for both girls and boys in a variety of different areas, such as technology, math and science, career education, and—you guessed it!—sports.

Before the passage of Title IX, only a small percentage of American girls—less than 5 percent—played high school sports. Neither high schools nor colleges budgeted much money for women's teams, although plenty of men's teams were well-funded. Title IX, which gave schools until July 1978 to meet its requirements, changed all of that. It brought an influx of funding for girl's and

Title IX has made it possible for generations of young female athletes to play volleyball on high school and college teams.

women's sports. Female students flocked to these new programs. In the years since the law passed, the number of girls playing high school sports grew by more than 1,000 percent, while the number of college women playing varsity sports increased by more than 600 percent.

While Title IX has seen some backlash—after all, money spent on women's sports means less money to spend on something else—it still has millions of supporters. It has opened up opportunities for generations of women. Credit for the growth of women's athletics belongs to more than just the existence of the law, though. As Title IX's coauthor and sponsor Senator Birch Bayh said, "those who made Title IX come alive are the coaches and the players and the parents. All of them participate in giving their daughters the same opportunities as their sons."

VOLLEYBALL BASICS

Volleyball is a sport that requires a lot of energy and a lot of teamwork. While the rules are complex, the basic concept is simple. Your team needs to keep the ball in the air and to send it over the net into the other team's side in a way that makes it difficult for them to do the same.

VOLLEYBALL HISTORY

Volleyball was invented in 1895 in Holyoke, Massachusetts. An instructor at a YMCA, William G. Morgan, wanted a game that combined elements of basketball, tennis, baseball, and handball. The sport was originally called mintonette, but the action of volleying the ball back and forth over the net gave it its current name, volleyball

Women have played volleyball for over one hundred years. These girls are playing at a Young Women's Christian Association (YWCA) camp in Idaho during the 1910s.

Since then the popularity of the sport has continued to rise. Indoor volleyball made its debut at the 1964 Olympics in Tokyo, Japan, and beach volleyball was made a medal sport at the 1996 Olympics in Atlanta, Georgia. It ranks as the third most played sport by American high school girls—after basketball and track and field. More than forty-six million Americans—men, women, and children—play volleyball in the United States today.

The women's game has come a long way since 1895, as well. The earliest reference for teaching the game to women, *Volleyball for Women* by Katherine M. Montgomery, was published in 1933. In 1952, the first Women's World Championships were held in

Moscow, and with the inclusion of volleyball in the 1964 Olympics, it was clear that women's volleyball was here to stay.

The 1970s was a productive decade for women in many ways, including their participation in the sport of volleyball. The year 1973, especially, was pivotal for women's volleyball. It was the inaugural year for both the Women's World Cup and the Junior World Championships. The twenty-six thousand spectators who came to watch the Women's World Championship in Brazil set a new record for attendance at a women's event.

Women's professional beach volleyball began to take off in the 1980s. In 1986, the Women's Professional Volleyball Association (WPVA) was created. In 1992, the FIVB (or Fédération Internationale de Volleyball, which is French for "International Federation of Volleyball") held its first women's beach volleyball competition in Almeria, Spain. The Association of Volleyball Professionals (AVP) started including women's events the following year. The WPVA ceased to exist after the 1997 season, but the FIVB and AVP continued to hold women's events. Thanks in part to the popularity of professional beach volleyball, beach volleyball was played at the Olympics for the first time in 1996.

Indoor volleyball hasn't had as much success at a professional level, unfortunately. The four-team United States Professional Volleyball League was launched in 2002, but sadly only lasted for a single season. The Premier Volleyball League, founded in 2012, met with a bit more success. The organization, which is sanctioned by USA Volleyball, has both both men's and women's teams

Despite the struggles of professional volleyball, the game has continued to grow in popularity with high school, college, and recreational players during the twenty-first century. The sport's future continues to look bright.

While it may be the newer branch of the sport, beach volleyball has become very popular in its own right. Lane Carico, seen here, is a professional beach volleyball player.

THE RULES OF THE GAME

Initially, volleyball consisted of nine innings and any number of players could play. The object was to serve and return the ball over the net, keeping it traveling from team to team without hitting the floor. If a team failed to return a serve, the serving team would score a point.

The rules have been refined over the years. Today, teams are made up of either two people (in beach volleyball) or six people (in indoor volleyball). The object of the game is to keep the ball from touching the ground or floor on your side of the court and then send it back to your opponent's side. Strategically, you want to send the ball over the net in such a way that it is difficult for your

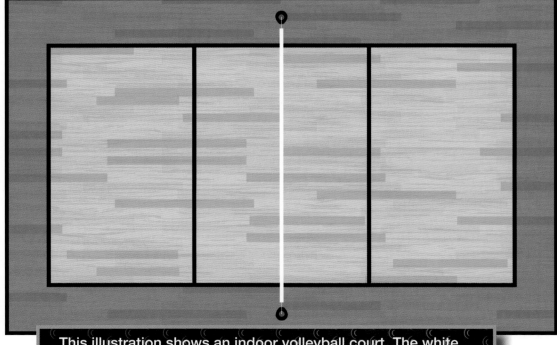

This illustration shows an indoor volleyball court. The white line down the middle is the net. The attack lines divide each side of the court into the back court and the front court.

opponent to return it. If they miss, can't return it, or send it out of bounds, your team will get a point or the serve (depending on how the game is being scored, which we will discuss shortly).

Spiking the ball is the most recognizable way to accomplish this goal. Each team can touch the ball only three times when it is on the team's side of the court (this includes blocking contact), and no player can touch the ball twice in a row unless she is blocking the ball at the net. (Blocking is singled out as an exception in the rules because it is not a manner of hitting the ball, like passing or spiking.)

BEACH VS. INDOOR VOLLEYBALL

	Beach	Indoor
Court Size	18 x 9 meters (19 x 9 yards)	16 x 8 meters (17 x 8 yards)
Court	Outdoors, on sand at least 40 centimeters (15 inches) deep	Indoors, a hardwood floor
Number of Sets per Game	Three	Five
Switching Sides	Teams switch sides every seven points in the first two sets and every five points in the third	Teams do not regularly switch sides.

HITTERS AND SETTERS

There are three basic strategies for indoor volleyball play: the 4-2, the 6-2, and the 5-1. The 4-2 is the most common set-up. It indicates a team with four hitters and two setters. The setters play opposite each other, meaning that if one setter is in the middle of the front row, the other is in the middle of the back row. In this configuration, one setter will always be in the front row to set for two hitters. The setter in the back row plays as a passer.

The 6-2 means that there are six hitters and two setters, but this does not mean that there are eight players on the court. It means that the two setters act as hitters as well. This is a little more complicated. After the ball is served, the setter in the back row moves to the front and the other setter remains in front, too, but moves to the right side of a hitter.

This means that there are four people in the front row and only two in the back. The goal of this set-up is to have most hitters and blockers in the front row. It is very important that every player knows where she is supposed to be; otherwise, the court will not be sufficiently covered.

The 5-1 is the most complicated strategy. It consists of five hitters and only one setter. The setter in this case does not do double duty as a hitter as well. In this strategy the setter must be fast, precise, and in very good shape. An advantage to this strategy is that the players get to know the setter's style; however, it can also leave the front row with only two hitters instead of three (like in the 6-2).

SCORING METHODS

Several systems of scoring are used in volleyball. The older method is called sideout scoring. In sideout scoring, only the team that is serving the ball can score a point. The nonserving team simply wins back the serve—and thus has the chance to score—if the serving team fails to return the ball in bounds. A team wins a set when it scores fifteen points with at least a two-point advantage. For example, a team can win if the score is 15-13, but not if the score is 15-14. In the event of a 16-16 tie, the team that scores the seventeenth point wins the set. The team that wins three sets (or, sometimes, the first five sets) first wins the game.

The other type of scoring is called rally-point scoring. It is the method that is most often used today. In rally-point scoring, the team that wins the rally (the back and forth of the ball) wins a point, regardless of whether that team served or not. And when the team wins the point, it also gains possession of the serve (if it did not already have it). The team that scores twenty-five points, with a two-point minimum advantage, wins each nondeciding set. In the deciding set, the victor is the first team that scores fifteen points with a two-point minimum advantage. With a rally-point scoring system, there is no scoring cap—meaning that the game continues for as long as is needed so that there is more than a one-point difference in the score.

TEAM MEMBERS

While individual volleyball team members may be excellent setters, spikers, or servers, every member of the team will have to set, spike, and serve. After all, each team member plays all the different areas of the court. Each time a team wins the serve, the players rotate one space clockwise, thus changing each player's position. While players physically rotate through positions on the floor, each skill position (the setter, hitter, or blocker) has certain strengths that the coach knows he or she can rely on.

You can't play volleyball without a volleyball! A regulation volleyball weighs about 10 ounces (0.3 kilograms).

Often, taller girls on the team are setters, blockers, and spikers. This is because they don't have to jump as high to reach the top of the net. Shorter girls also can play these positions if they have explosive jumping power. Jump training is something that can help you become an effective blocker.

Good hitters are both agile and stable. It doesn't matter if you are short or tall, as long as you can sense where the ball is directed and make sure you can get under it to pass it to your setter. As we'll discuss later, there are many ways for you to work on your coordination and agility.

GETTING INVOLVED

It doesn't have to cost a lot to play volleyball. All you need is a pair of volleyball shoes and a volleyball. Regulation size and weight volleyballs come in both leather and vinyl. Volleyballs start at around $15, though high-end volleyballs more commonly sell for between $60 and $80. When getting shoes, you need a combination of cushioning, stability, and lateral—or side-to-side—support. Shoes come in high-, medium-, and low-top. Many major athletic footwear makers make specific volleyball shoes, and prices start at around $60.

There are usually many opportunities to get involved in volleyball through your school. Volleyball is often offered in gym class, where the basic positions and rules are explained and practiced. Many schools also have their own teams that play other schools for standings in an organized, official league. Schools might also have club teams, which are more informally organized and often do not require tryouts. Playing on these more casual teams gives you a great opportunity to learn the game and get experience so you will have the skills needed to make your school team.

If your school doesn't offer volleyball, you might try the local YWCA or community center. You can contact the US Youth Volleyball League to learn where the teams are in your area. The regional office of USA Volleyball also has a list of club teams.

CHAPTER TWO

VOLLEYBALL SKILLS

If you want to be a good volleyball player, you'll need to spend a lot of time working on your skills. It's not enough to just be a good spiker. Every player on the team should have strong skills in each area. It can take years of practice and experience to develop top-rate volleyball skills. One thing to remember is that all movement and action should start from the ready position—feet apart, knees bent, eyes forward, ready to move in any direction.

SERVING THE BALL

Serving is the action that gets the ball going. It is a common way to score points because many times a serve can be so powerful that the opponent can't return it. When you score a point like this, it's called an "ace." The overhand serve is the one most often seen

This young player is serving the ball. Serving is one of the most basic volleyball skills. There are both underhand and overhand styles of serving.

the Olympics and professional sports. Standing at the end line, toss the ball 2 to 3 feet (61 to 91 cm) above your head and slightly in front of you. Make sure you don't touch the end line before making contact with the ball—otherwise, you will lose the serve. Take a step forward while shifting your weight from your right to left foot, if you are right-handed. Arch your back and bend your right arm to bring it up from behind your head. Hit the ball with your hand and make sure your arm follows through.

The first way to work on your serve is to practice the form as outlined above. Once you get the hang of it, try choosing a target and directing your serve toward it. For a greater challenge, put a time limit on yourself—see how many good serves you can do in a minute.

PASSING AND SETTING

When receiving a serve, you'll need to know how to pass or "bump" the ball. When bumping, you want to place the ball high enough for a teammate to set it so that a third hitter can spike it. In making a good pass you can set up a play that might win you a point or the serve.

When you pass, the ball hits the widest part of your forearm, right between the wrist and elbow. Don't swing your arms at the ball. Instead, move your arms by shrugging your shoulders in the direction you want the ball to go.

You can hold your hands in three different ways. You can cup them together and cross your thumbs in the center. You can make a fist with your writing hand and put your other hand over it, making sure that both thumbs are touching and side by side. Or, you can lay one hand into the palm of the other and cross your thumbs. Your thumbs are important because if they are in the right position, your arms are in the right position.

Passing may not be the flashiest skill in volleyball, but it is arguably the most important one. Proper hand placement is important when passing.

A simple drill for working on your bump is to bump the ball repeatedly off your own arms. You can also get a couple of team-mates together to play "keep it up," passing the ball from player to player without letting it drop or having to set it, which leads us to our next type of pass.

Setting is an overhand pass. You should start in the ready position facing where you want the ball to go. With your hands above your head and your fingers spread, make a triangle with them by having your thumbs and index fingers touch. You don't want your hands too far above your head, just slightly above and in front of your face. Make sure that you get underneath the ball and that your elbows and knees are bent. When the ball touches your fingers, extend your arms and legs to move the ball.

Make sure that both hands touch the ball at the same time; otherwise, the referee might count it as a double or a mishandle. A double could result in your team losing possession of the ball if you have the serve or in your opponents being awarded a point if they have the serve. Also, don't let the ball touch the palm of your hand—otherwise, you will be called for "pushing," which is a way of controlling the ball unfairly.

You can practice the skill of setting by doing a variation of the "keep it up" drill. Try lying on your back with your arms extended upward and your elbows facing outward. Set the ball upwards and see how long you can do it. You can do this standing as well.

SPIKING THE BALL

One of the more difficult, but useful, skills to acquire is hitting, more commonly known as spiking. Spiking is a quick offensive movement. Done properly, it is a difficult or impossible hit to return. A setter will position the ball so that you, the spiker, can take a couple

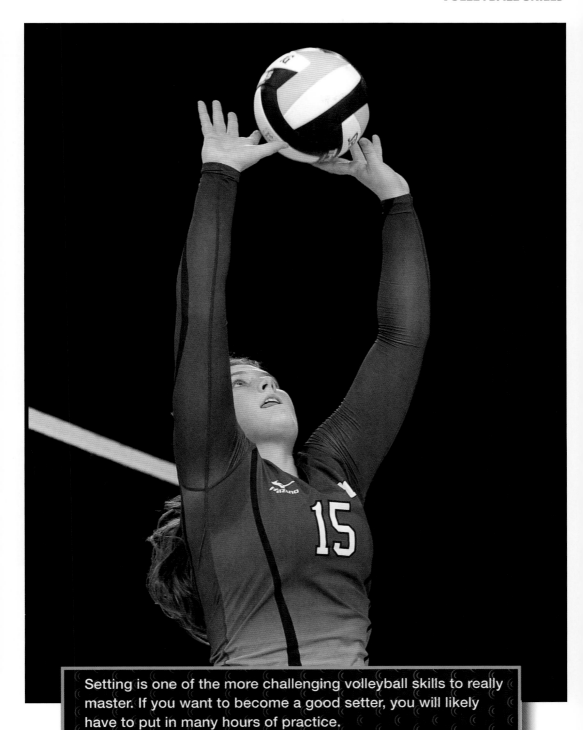

Setting is one of the more challenging volleyball skills to really master. If you want to become a good setter, you will likely have to put in many hours of practice.

THE GREAT FLO HYMAN

Flora "Flo" Hyman (1954–1986) was one of the greatest volleyball players in the history of the game. Known not only for her excellent spiking and defensive skills, but also for her personality and charm, she was the first American woman to be voted to the All-World Cup volleyball team. An all-around player, the 6-foot, 5-inch (195 cm) Hyman led the US Women's Olympic team to a silver medal in the 1984 Olympics.

After the Olympics, she went to Japan to play professional volleyball there. During a match in 1986, she collapsed and died. She was just thirty-one. Her death was a result of Marfan's syndrome, a genetic heart disorder that predominantly affects tall, thin individuals.

Hyman was inducted into the Volleyball Hall of Fame in 1988. Her dedication to female athletes in all sports led the Women's Sports Foundation to name the Flo Hyman Memorial Award after her. It was awarded annually between 1987 and 2004 to athletes who captured Hyman's "dignity, spirit, and commitment to excellence."

of steps forward and then jump up with both feet. As you jump, you should swing both arms forward. Pull your hitting arm back with the elbow and hand around shoulder height. Your hand should be open, not in a fist. As you swing your hand and arm over your head, the heel of your hand will make contact first, followed by your palm, and then fingers (which snap through the ball). Your contact point should be just in front of your hitting shoulder and as high as possible.

Spiking is best practiced by having a partner repeatedly set the ball for you. It can also be done as a group drill with one person setting and the rest coming up, one after another, to spike.

One of the best ways to stop a spike is by blocking. To be a good blocker, a good sense of timing and strong jumping legs are essential. To develop your blocking skills, make sure that you keep your eye on the spiker. You'll have to watch her eyes, shoulders, and hands to figure out when and where she's going to spike. You don't

Spiking the ball is one of the most recognizable volleyball moves. The player who spikes the ball is usually, but not always, in the front row.

want to jump too soon and miss your opportunity. Stand close to the net, but not so close that you touch it. When you sense she's about to spike, jump straight up from both feet with your arms extended upward. If your timing is right, the ball will bounce straight back into your opponent's court. If you're not quite that successful, you'll slow the ball down enough so that one of your teammates can get to it.

The only way to develop the sense of timing that will make you a great blocker is through practice. That said, you can always work on your jumping. If there is a net that you can use, practice approaching it with a couple of steps and then jumping as though you were going to block the ball. Another drill is to jump upward as if to block, shooting your arms above, and repeating that action as many times in a row as possible. As soon as you touch the ground, jump up again. With each jump, you should be reaching above the volleyball net. Once you can no longer reach that high, stop.

CHAPTER THREE

STAYING HEALTHY

Along with practicing specific skills, you need to work on your general conditioning and fitness, which will enhance your ability to perform. Without strong legs, how will you jump high? Without strong arms, how will you hit the ball powerfully? And without endurance, how will you play strong for the entire game? An average game can last anywhere from sixty to ninety minutes and, while players aren't in constant motion, they do need to be ready to perform well throughout that entire time. Developing overall endurance, both muscular and cardiovascular, is an important step in training for volleyball.

Cardiovascular enduran60ce means that your heart can deliver blood to your muscles and that your muscles can use it efficiently and quickly. Any activity that keeps your heart rate up for at least twenty minutes at a time, like running or rollerblading, is a good

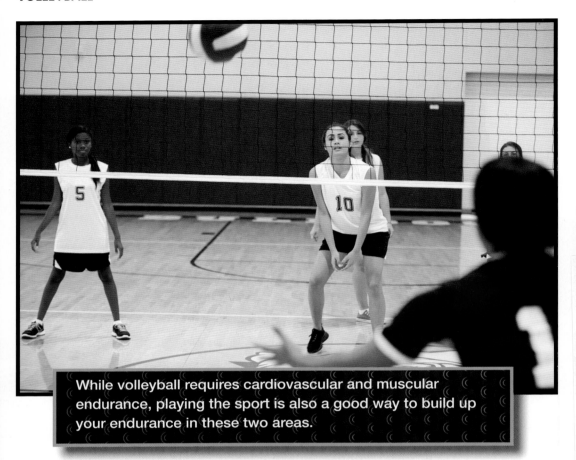

While volleyball requires cardiovascular and muscular endurance, playing the sport is also a good way to build up your endurance in these two areas.

way to develop that kind of endurance. Working on your cardiovascular conditioning three times a week is a good formula for increased endurance.

Developing muscle endurance increases your muscles' ability to perform an action continuously over an extended period of time, and allows you to give your all, over and over. Volleyball requires not only sustained effort, like that required for moving around on the court, but also short bursts of action, like jumping to block or spike the ball. Cycling, swimming, or running will help your muscles develop sustained endurance, while practicing your jumping will help enable your muscles to perform quick actions repeatedly.

BEYOND ENDURANCE

It's not all about endurance, though. You also need strength, flexibility, and coordination (which includes balance and agility, the ability to move quickly and gracefully).

An overall strength-training program, which includes working your arms, legs, and upper body, can help you in many ways. To develop a good weight-lifting program, consult with your coach or a trainer at your gym.

Flexibility allows your body to perform a wide range of movement and helps you stay injury-free. People who can bend at the waist and touch their hands to the floor have a nice degree of flexibility. Incorporating a stretching regimen or yoga into your training will help increase your range of motion.

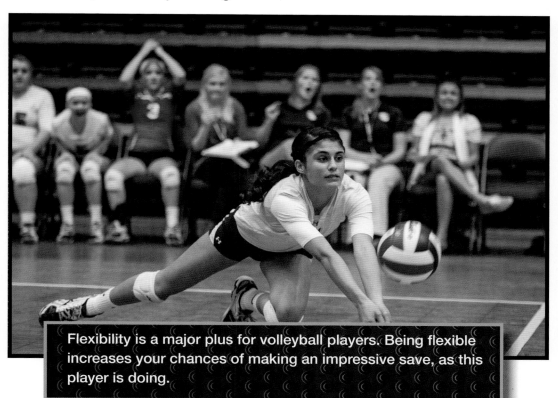

Flexibility is a major plus for volleyball players. Being flexible increases your chances of making an impressive save, as this player is doing.

Coordination is very important in volleyball. Often, you will have to sprint to get to the ball while preparing to return it and, hopefully, seeing a good place to direct it. That's a lot of different things going on at the same time. Coordination makes it possible for you to do all those things. Agility is the ability to change your direction of movement quickly, like sprinting to the ball and then back to position to be ready again. Balance allows you to stay on your feet.

STRETCHING

Stretching is a critical part of any conditioning regimen. Stretching primes your muscles for the workout ahead, which helps prevent injuries that stem from putting too much stress on unprepared or already tight or fatigued muscles.

Proper stretching begins after you have warmed your muscles up and raised your heart rate. You can run for a few minutes, do some jumping jacks, or jump rope to get the blood flowing. The following are just a few exercises you can do to stretch your muscles and get ready to play. Hold the stretches consistently for about thirty seconds. Don't bounce. Repeat each of them at least twice on each side.

Calf Muscles

Find a wall, a tree, or some other sturdy structure. Stand about 2 feet (61 cm) away from it. Step back about 1 foot (30 cm) with your right foot. Bend your left knee and lean forward, pushing slightly on the wall in front of you. Your right leg should be straight and you should feel a stretch in the right calf. If you need to, you can move you left foot forward a bit to get more of a stretch. Hold this for thirty seconds and then switch feet.

Hamstrings

Sit on the floor with your right leg extended and your left leg bent under you, with your foot touching your buttocks. Slowly begin to slide your hands down the straight leg. You should start to feel a stretch in the back of that leg. Hold this position for thirty seconds. Don't round your lower back; try to keep it fairly straight, bending at the waist. Return to a sitting position when done. Switch sides and repeat.

Quadriceps

Stand with your hips facing forward, bend your right knee back, and grab your right ankle with your right hand. Keep your hips facing forward and your right knee pointing at the floor. You should feel a mild stretch along the front of your right leg. Hold this for thirty seconds and then switch legs.

Your Shoulders

Since your shoulders will see a lot of action in a volleyball game, it is not a bad idea to do both of the stretches outlined here before you begin practicing. You should feel this first stretch in your shoulder. Rotate your shoulders forward (like shrugging) ten times and then backward ten times. The second stretch is great for your triceps. Raise your right arm. Then bend it at the elbow so that your right hand is behind your head and your right elbow is pointing toward the sky. Take your left hand and gently pull your right elbow further behind your head, toward the left. Let your right hand slide down your back. Keep your shoulders down and relaxed. When you begin to feel the stretch in your muscle, hold for thirty seconds. Then switch arms.

DEALING WITH INJURIES

Although volleyball is not a dangerous activity, it can lead to injuries. Injuries suffered by volleyball players usually occur in the ankles, knees, shoulders, or lower back.

Knee and Ankle Injuries

When two or three players make contact or collide, it's not uncommon for one of them to come away with a knee or ankle injury. This generally happens near or underneath the net. As players scramble to take or resume positions, paths sometimes cross and bodies fall. You can also pull or tear muscles and ligaments while diving for the ball.

As far as your choice of shoes, there is no clear-cut case for the low,- mid-, or high-top when it comes to prevention. Some players will wear some kind of ankle support. Almost 85 percent of all sprains result from falling on the outside of the foot, causing the sole to turn inward.

There are three degrees of sprains. The first involves the stretching of ligaments. These are usually mild and you'll experience some pain, point tenderness, swelling, and limited disability. The second degree is more serious, as it involves the tearing of the ligaments. You will feel more pain and be limited in your movement. You won't be able to put any weight on the ankle. The third degree, and most serious, is when the ligaments are ruptured. Severe pain, joint instability, and disability are just some of the signs. A doctor should attend to second and third degree sprains.

Any ankle sprain will bruise and swell within twenty-four hours. Remember "RICE"—rest, ice, compression, and elevation—and you'll aid your own recovery. Be sure to ice any ankle sprain regularly

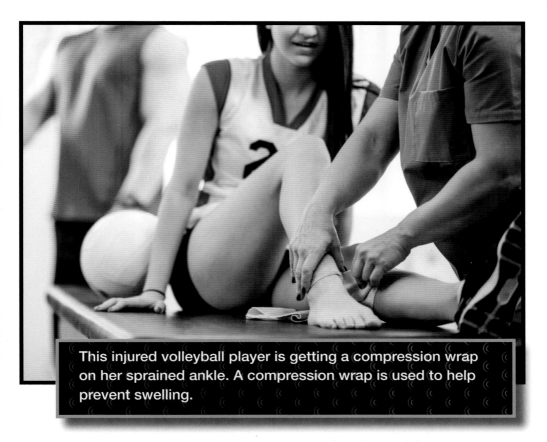

This injured volleyball player is getting a compression wrap on her sprained ankle. A compression wrap is used to help prevent swelling.

in twenty-minute increments during the first forty-eight to seventy-two hours. How long you must rest depends upon the severity of the sprain. If you feel minor discomfort and can walk on it after twenty-four hours, you might be able to practice your setting or passing, but don't go too fast or you'll likely increase the damage. Unfortunately, once you hurt your ankle it's often susceptible to more injuries. To keep your ankle from reinjury, you might consider wearing an ankle brace to add stability.

The other major joint injury occurs in the knees. Knee injuries come not only from contact with other players, but from the repeated running, jumping, and turning that players do during a game. Falling on your knees to get a ball can also cause a strain. Knees are very complicated joints, and any injury or pain in them should be treated seriously. Some players will wear kneepads or braces to help avoid knee injuries.

Shoulder and Back Injuries

Your shoulders will see a lot of action in a volleyball game. Good conditioning, strength training, and stretching can help prevent injuries in the shoulder area. However, even then, not everyone can avoid getting hurt. Some of the symptoms of a shoulder injury are a numbing pain throughout the arm, unusual sounds (like cracking or popping) when you rotate your shoulder, pain when doing something simple like throwing a ball, and an inability to raise your arm above ninety degrees.

Doctors can treat shoulder injuries in a number of ways, depending upon the severity. One thing is certain, though, shoulder injuries require a lot of rest—anywhere from eight to ten weeks or more. You might also get a rehabilitation program set up for you by a physical therapist. This can help you gradually regain full use and movement in your shoulder.

Lower back injuries stem from the repeated stress placed on that area (the lumbar spine) by spiking and serving. This area bears the weight of your body as you move, and the arching and the twisting of the back can result in injury. Lower back injuries may manifest as spasms, pinched nerves, or herniated discs. If you experience back pain and it doesn't go away within a day or so, see your doctor.

The Importance of Treatment

All of these injuries can be serious if not treated carefully. It doesn't make you a tougher athlete if you suffer silently through pain, all the while making your injury worse. Many female athletes feel like they have to prove that they are tough. In reality, it takes a smart and strong woman to listen to her body and do what's right for it.

If you do experience injury, it can be a time to appreciate volleyball from the sidelines. You can watch how your team performs, support them, and think about how your contribution can improve. Also, use this time to explore other parts of your life so that you are refreshed and hungry to play by the time you have healed.

DON'T OVERDO IT

Injuries are not the only event that can sideline you; overtraining is another aspect of sports that can keep you out of the game. It is not uncommon for enthusiasm and the desire to improve to lead to too much training. That is why part of being a good athlete is being able to listen to your body and know when it needs rest and attention.

There is a limit to your body's ability to adapt to and endure training, especially when you increase the intensity. Your body needs rest and time to recover after hard workouts. Muscles need to rebuild and flush out toxins. Overtraining can occur when your level of intensity is too high too early in your training. It can happen when you don't give yourself enough time to rest or when you train without considering other stresses in your life. Maybe your workouts aren't getting more difficult but you have a big term paper due in a week. All stresses in your life affect your body and your training. When you overload your body with stress, you are prone to overtraining. And overtraining can be as detrimental to your performance and progress as injuries.

If you overtrain, you'll feel tired, you won't be able to play as well as you did before, and you will feel as though there is nothing more you can do. The harder you train, the slower you'll seem to get. The only way to recuperate is by resting. You don't have to

Sitting on the sidelines during a game may not be your idea of fun, but going back into the game while you are injured is a surefire way to make your injury worse.

be totally inactive, but you should try something different and less stressful on your body, such as leisurely bike rides, swimming, or taking long walks.

THE RIGHT MINDSET

Just as your body needs conditioning to perform well, so does your mind. For years, professional athletes have used visualization and goal setting as tools to help them perform better. If you're physically prepared but your head is not in the game, you will not perform your best.

First of all, it is important to have a good attitude. Approach volleyball with a desire to learn and improve. It's tough not to compare yourself to others, but you should concentrate on just doing the best that you can do. When you give your all, you should be happy with yourself, even if your team didn't win the game or someone else played better.

If you are having difficulty with a particular move or skill, it often helps to think about it, to visualize it. Imagine yourself executing a great overhand serve. One of the benefits of visualization is that you can slow down, repeat, or even stop the action in your head. This allows you to think about how you stand, the position of the ball in the air, how you make contact, and the final follow-through. By visualizing it, you can learn it mentally and then put it into practice physically.

Setting goals is also a great mental exercise. By setting goals you can help yourself stay motivated. Goal setting also helps by focusing your attention and relieving stress. You can set goals for yourself as well as for your team. Maybe you want to perfect your overhand serve, and you want to help the team communicate better. These are two very realistic goals. You can work on your serve

Setting small-scale goals can help you make your way toward large-scale goals, such as winning your town or state's volleyball championship.

through practice and visualization, and you can foster communication on your team by communicating yourself.

Make sure that your goals are realistic. If you have long-term goals like being on the starting lineup, make sure you have some intermediate ones as well that will both help you reach your long-term goal and give you a sense of satisfaction and accomplishment along the way. Maybe what you need to get on the starting lineup is that overhand serve.

Finally, set goals for yourself in the other areas of your life. This helps establish a balance. Setting goals for school or other activities helps keep things in perspective. Achieving balance isn't always easy, particularly when you're excited about something new, such as volleyball. But balance allows you to focus on other things that are important in your life—like friends, school, family, and other hobbies. It's great to give your new interest your all, but the other areas of your life shouldn't have to suffer. Spending time away from volleyball is also important because it gives you both a physical and a mental break. A break can take the shape of a holiday or playing a different sport in the off-season. When you take a break and then return to play, you're refreshed. If you don't do other things, too, volleyball can become mundane and even feel like a chore.

EATING RIGHT

How many times have you heard that your body is like a machine and needs fuel? Well, it's true, and the right kind of fuel can help your body perform better and longer. A soda and a doughnut might help you make it through the morning, but once the initial sugar-and-caffeine rush wears off, you will be groggy and tired again.

Nutritionists don't all agree on the best diet. Some favor a diet high in carbohydrates, such as pasta, grains, and bread. Others prefer a diet high in protein from foods such as fish, meat, legumes (beans), and nuts. As a growing woman and

It's a lot easier to eat right when you keep a variety of healthy foods around the house. Apples make a quick and easy snack.

EATING DISORDERS

Unfortunately, it's common for women athletes to become obsessed with their weight and body size. In a sport like volleyball, girls often feel self-conscious because of the fairly revealing uniforms. This can result in what is known as the female athlete triad—eating disorders, low bone density, and missed periods. These three things can develop when you try to control your eating in such a way that you don't get enough nutrients. Being healthy and strong are two of the most important things for an athlete. Poor eating habits or eating disorders destroy both.

athlete, it's best to make sure you get a good balance of both of these, along with dairy products and plenty of fruits and vegetables. While dairy products are a great source of calcium, there are some people whose bodies are not able to process milk. If you are lactose-intolerant, you should stick with soy milk and other lactose-free products.

Women need lots of calcium to help build bone mass, especially because many women suffer from osteoporosis, a loss of bone density that causes bones to become brittle and break easily—and it's not something that just happens to "old ladies." Whether you get your calcium from a glass of milk, some soy yogurt, or calcium supplements, it's important to get enough (one thousand milligrams per day for young women between the ages of nine and eighteen, according to the National Institutes of Health).

Following a balanced diet will ensure that you get all the nutrients your body needs. Neglect an area like vegetables and you'll miss out on a great source of vitamins and minerals. Protein, which can be found in soy products and meat, will help build and repair tissue, as well as provide vitamins and minerals. And grains are an excellent source of fiber and carbohydrates for energy.

It's also important to drink lots of water. Your body is made up of water more than anything else, and you need to keep it that way. Dehydration can be a very serious problem for athletes. Water keeps you going and keeps your system functioning smoothly. Athletes need to drink even more water than people who are less active because of the large amount of water that they lose through sweating.

CHAPTER FOUR

PLAYING ON A TEAM

W hile perfecting your skills and staying healthy can be satisfying in and of themselves, they are things that volleyball players do, at least in part, to win games. Volleyball is very much a team sport, and one of the biggest joys the game offers is working with your teammates to win a game.

HEALTHY COMPETITION

We all want to win, and that desire is often what motivates us to work our hardest. Competition is a healthy aspect of sports, as long as you learn to take it in stride and keep it in perspective.

Keeping competition in perspective means realizing that the outcome of the game is not entirely under your control. Sometimes, even when you work hard and play well, you don't win. It is important

Volleyball can be a very competitive sport. While it is good to develop a competitive edge, you don't want to become unhealthily competitive.

to focus on the process of competing rather than just on the outcome. Focus on what you and the team did well, and praise others and yourself for a job well done. Also, be aware of where you or the team did not do well, and focus on improving those weaknesses when you are at practice.

In volleyball, you may face competition once a week at a scheduled match, or during a weekend tournament where you play a number of games in a series of elimination rounds. It's important to prepare for every game. Make sure that you're well rested the day before. Don't have a long conditioning session or increase your weights right before a game. Your muscles will be too busy recuperating for you to give it your all. You can still do an easy workout. Your coach will probably arrange to have your workouts follow this plan, but you also must know what works best for you. You need to pay attention to your body and know how to prepare yourself to perform your best on game day.

Mentally, you will need to relax. Focus on your own performance within the team. Don't stress yourself out by worrying about what you can't do or how you might mess up. Instead, think about doing everything to the best of your ability. Remember how you've set the ball for your teammates or how well you served in other matches in the past.

TRUSTING YOUR TEAMMATES

Keep in mind that you are part of a team. If a team works as a unit, it can go much farther and be much more successful than any individual alone. Liz Masakayan, a professional women's beach volleyball player, sums it up when she says, "A volleyball team is a lot like a marriage: It requires trust, responsibility, and problem solving. It's an intense bond you have with your teammates: You work, travel, and room together, and as in any relationship, there are problems that need to be solved."

To work as a team, players need to be able to communicate and trust each other. When a serve comes to your side, a player should call for it and others should be confident in the player's ability and not second-guess her. If the setter is in position, she should communicate to her teammates so that they'll pass to her. Communicate not just to direct and claim, but also to encourage each other.

GETTING ALONG WITH TEAMMATES

You may not always get along with all of your teammates. Nobody says you have to be best friends, but you should try to respect each other. At the very least, it's important to keep the lines of

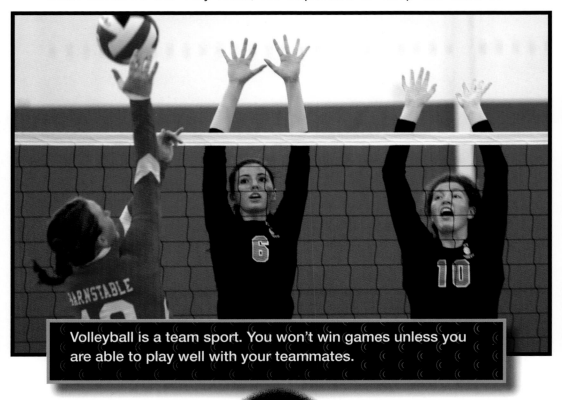

Volleyball is a team sport. You won't win games unless you are able to play well with your teammates.

communication open. You might need your coach to help two members of the team who won't talk to each other. It's normal for there to be disagreements or disappointments, but they shouldn't hang over you too long. Letting conflicts stew affects the entire team. You could end up dreading practice or games. Conflict is natural—deal with it.

You might also experience conflict with your coach. Think about what the basis of your conflict is—do you think he or she is pushing you too hard? Does he or she say things about your performance that make you mad? Do the two of you disagree about strategy? You don't have to think that your coach is the greatest, but you should respect him or her. A coach's job is to bring out the best in each player and to bring all of the players on the team together. Sometimes harsh words are spoken, but the intention usually isn't

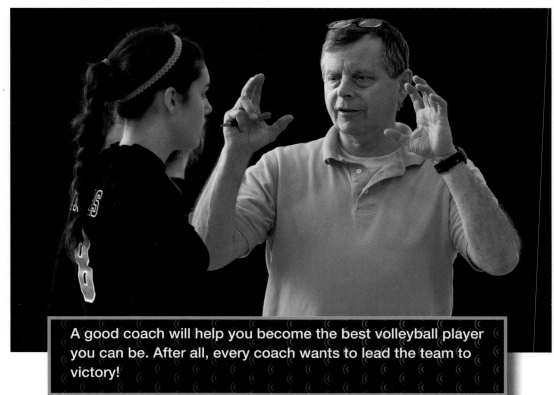

A good coach will help you become the best volleyball player you can be. After all, every coach wants to lead the team to victory!

to hurt. If you feel like comments are inappropriate or wrong, talk to your coach. Maybe the coach does not realize that his or her comments were hurtful. Conflict is almost always best dealt with by communicating. By confronting the situation, you may be able to come to a peaceable understanding.

Competition is a great part of team sports, especially when everyone is working together and keeping their focus on playing the game. Every team has its share of wins and losses, but every athlete is a winner when she plays to the best of her abilities.

WINNING ISN'T EVERYTHING

It's easy to get caught up in the spirit of the moment and become so focused on winning that you forget about being a good sport. You may want to hate your opponents and say some nasty things to her, but she's out there just like you, and she, too, is doing her best. Good sportsmanship means focusing on doing your best, enjoying the game, and enjoying the competition. Calling a girl on the other team an "ugly cheater" does nothing to enhance your own performance. It brings you down, as well. Instead, let an opponent's tough play inspire you to play better.

Good sportsmanship doesn't always prevail, and trouble can brew between opposing teams. The best thing to do is just walk away. You might be angry at a loss or you might be celebrating loudly over a win, but saying something rude or gloating to an opposing player doesn't help make the loss easier or the victory sweeter.

PLAYING PROFESSIONALLY

While there are far more opportunities to pursue your interest in volleyball in high school or college, it is possible to do so professionally,

COLLEGE VOLLEYBALL

There are plenty of opportunities for women to play volleyball in college. The passage of Title IX ensured greater scholarship opportunities for women athletes all over the country. There are more than 1,700 colleges and universities that have NCAA teams, and more than 300 of those are Division I teams. There are actually more women's volleyball teams than men's volleyball teams at the collegiate level— more than ten times as many, in fact.

Being a good volleyball player in high school can help you get into college—and even help you pay for it! Women's volleyball scholarships are offered at schools across the country, from Ivy League colleges to state universities.

too. There are professional, national, and international leagues for both beach and indoor volleyball. The USA Premier Volleyball League draws teams from forty regional volleyball associations across the United States. It started out with twelve women's teams during its first season, in 2012. The following year, several men's teams and three more women's teams were added. The league holds a championship each year.

Beach volleyball players also have professional opportunities available to them. Women's professional beach volleyball is organized by the AVP in the United States. International beach volleyball events are organized by the FIVB. Both host and arrange tournaments and competitive events for both male and female beach volleyball players.

Some professional volleyball players play for teams overseas. For example, the American player Jordan Larson has played for clubs in Russia and Turkey.

PLAYING FOR FUN

You don't have to be a professional player to continue playing as an adult. There are plenty of recreational leagues for adults. Recreational leagues do not lack for competition or commitment to the sport, so you don't have to worry about losing your edge. A love of the game developed now can last well into your adult life.

Volleyball can help you develop your body, your understanding of teamwork, and your sense of competition and achievement. Keeping strong and healthy in both your mind and body is something that will benefit you throughout your life, and volleyball can help you accomplish these things. You don't have to wait for another gym class to try volleyball again, you can go out and make your own opportunity. It's a great sport, and you won't regret giving it a try.

TIMELINE

1895 Volleyball is invented in Holyoke, Massachusetts.

1920s Beach volleyball gets its start in Santa Monica, California.

1964 Volleyball makes its first official appearance in the Olympic Games

1965 The California Beach Volleyball Association is founded.

1970 The United States' Mary Jo Peppier is voted the out-standing volleyball player in the world at the International Games in Bulgaria.

1975 Olympian and US national team member Debbie Green becomes volleyball's youngest All-American at sixteen years of age.

1975 Mary Jo Peppier is named the International Volleyball Association's Coach of the Year.

1983 The Association of Volleyball Professionals (AVP) is formed. It is a beach volleyball league.

1984 The US women's volleyball team wins its first Olympic medal, a silver.

1986 The Women's Professional Volleyball Association (WPVA) is created.

1987 The first Women's Professional Volleyball event is held in Newport Beach, CA, on May 16–17.

1987 Tennis player Martina Navratilova is honored as the first recipient of the Women's Sports Foundation's Flo Hyman Award, given by the Women's Sports Foundation in honor of the captain of the 1984 Olympic Silver Medalist United States Women's Volleyball Team.

1993 The FIVB Women's World Championship Series is initiated. The AVP also holds its first women's events.

1995 Players celebrate the sport of volleyball's centennial, or hundredth anniversary.

1996 Beach volleyball is played as an Olympic Sport for the first time.

1999 Eight new women's events are introduced at the Pan American Games in Winnipeg, Manitoba: soccer, weightlifting, shooting, pole vaulting, hammer throw, modern pentathalon, water polo, and beach volleyball.

2000 Beach Volleyball America (BVA), a women's professional organization, begins its first season.

2001 After just one year, the BVA folds.

2002 The United States Professional Volleyball League is founded (and lasts just one season.)

2008 The NCAA announces changes to the rules for women's volleyball at the college level, including changes in scoring.

2011 Misty May-Treanor and Kerri Walsh become the first women's team to win one hundred beach volleyball tournament titles.

2012 The Premier Volleyball League is founded. In its first year it consists of twelve women's volleyball teams.

2013 The first men's teams join the Premier Volleyball League.

GLOSSARY

CARDIOVASCULAR Having to do with the heart and blood vessels.

COMPRESSION Squeezing or pressing together.

CONDITIONING Getting physically ready.

DEFENSE A plan or action to keep the opposing team from scoring.

DEHYDRATION Not having enough water in one's body.

ENDURANCE Withstanding long periods of stress.

FEDERAL Having to do with the national government.

LATERAL Pertaining to side-to-side movement.

LIGAMENT The tissue that joins bones or cartilage, or supports organs and muscles.

MOTIVATION An incentive or psychological push.

MUSCLES Tissues that allow a body to move.

NUTRIENTS Substances found in foods that nourish the body.

OFFENSIVE The means used in an attempt to score.

RECUPERATE To restore health and strength.

REHABILITATION To restore regular activity after an injury.

SANCTION To officially allow or approve.

SCHOLARSHIP Financial aid given to students.

STABILITY Resistance to sudden change or action.

STRATEGY Planning; a plan of action.

VISUALIZATION Forming a mental picture or image.

VOLLEY To toss or hit something back and forth quickly.

FOR MORE INFORMATION

Association of Volleyball Professionals (AVP)
1300 Quail Street, #200
Newport Beach, CA 92660
(949) 679-3599
Website: http://avp.com
Founded in 1983, the AVP is the main organization for beach
   volleyball players in the United States. It holds the AVP Pro
   Beach Volleyball Tour and hosts beach volleyball events
   around the country.

California Beach Volleyball Association (CBVA)
28925 Pacific Coast Highway, #101
Malibu, CA 90265
(310) 457-8451
Website: www.cbva.com
This organization holds tournaments for beach volleyball players at multiple locations in the state of California. It offers
   tournaments at several different levels (such as AAA, AA,
   and A) and hosts men's, women's, and coed events.

Canadian Collegiate Athletic Association (CCAA)
2 St. Lawrence Drive
Cornwall, ON K6H 4Z1
Canada
(705) 742-1590
Website: http://www.ccaa.ca/women-s-s14844

Women's Volleyball is one of several sports in which the CCAA holds national championships. The current form of the National Women's Volleyball Championship is a competition between Canada's top eight women's college volleyball teams.

Fédération Internationale de Volleyball (FIVB)
Château Les Tourelles
Ch. Edouard-Sandoz 2-4
1006 Lausanne
Switzerland
+41 21 345 35 35
Website: http://www.fivb.com
This international organization was formed by representatives from fourteen nations in 1947. Today, it has 220 affiliated organizations and holds events around the world. Though it initially focused on indoor volleyball, the group now also holds beach volleyball events.

The National Collegiate Athletic Association (NCAA)
700 West Washington Street
PO Box 6222
Indianapolis, IN 46206
(317) 917-6222
Website: http://www.ncaa.com/sports/volleyball-women
The NCAA is responsible for setting the rules for competitive sports at the college level, as well as for holding tournaments and championships. The organization has teams in three divisions. Its member include more than 1,700 schools with women's volleyball teams.

United States Youth Volleyball League (USYVL)
2771 Plaza Del Amo
Torrance, CA 90503
(310) 212-7008
Website: https://www.usyvl.org
The aim of this organization is to provide opportunities for kids
between the ages of seven and fifteen to play volleyball in a
safe, supportive environment. The group has youth leagues
in all fifty US states.

USA Volleyball
4065 Sinton Road, Suite 200
Colorado Springs, CO 80907
(719) 228-6800
Website: http://www.teamusa.org/USA-Volleyball
As the national governing body for volleyball in the United
States, this nonprofit organization works to promote and
popularize the sport. It tries to recruit players to the sport
and has played a key role in training American volleyball
teams for the Olympic Games. The group also puts out the
magazine *VolleyballUSA*.

Volleyball Canada
1084 Kenaston Street, Unit 1A
Ottawa, ON K1B 3P5
Canada
613-748-5681
Website: http://www.volleyball.ca
This national organization is dedicated to the growth of volley-
ball in Canada. The group's website features contact

information for the associations in each of the country's provinces and territories, as well as information about how to play the game.

WEBSITES

Because of the changing nature of Internet links, Rosen Publishing has developed an online list of websites related to the subject of this book. This site is updated regularly. Please use this link to access the list:

http://www.rosenlinks.com/IX/Volley

FOR FURTHER READING

American Volleyball Coaches Association. *The Volleyball Drill Book*. Champaign, IL: Human Kinetics, 2012.

Cambridge Recruiting Review. *Guide to Women's Volleyball Colleges: Detailed Profiles on 1,272 NCAA & NAIA Volleyball Schools.* New York, NY: Cambridge Review, 2015.

Crisfield, Deborah W., and John Monteleone. *Winning Volleyball for Girls* (Winning Sports for Girls). New York, NY: Chelsea House Publishers, 2009.

Crockett, Kyle A. *Nutrition for Achievement in Sports and Academics* (Understanding Nutrition: a Gateway to Physical and Mental Health). Broomall, PA: Mason Crest, 2013.

Doeden, Matt. *Volleyball* (Summer Olympic Sports). Mankato, MN: Amicus Publishing, 2015.

Fay, Gail. *Sports: The Ultimate Teen Guide* (It Happened to Me). Lanham, MD: Scarecrow Press, 2012.

Hebert, Mike. *Thinking Volleyball*. Champaign, IL: Human Kinetics, 2013.

Kenny, Bonnie, and Cindy Gregory. *Volleyball: Steps to Success*. Champaign, IL: Human Kinetics, 2006.

May-Treanor, Misty, and Jill Lieber Steeg. *Misty: My Journey Through Volleyball and Life*. New York, NY: Scribner, 2011.

McIntyre, Abigail. *An Insider's Guide to Volleyball* (Sports Tips, Techniques, and Strategies). New York, NY: Rosen Classroom, 2014.

Oldenburg, Steve. *Complete Conditioning for Volleyball*. Champaign, IL: Human Kinetics, 2014.

Schmidt, Becky. *Volleyball: Steps to Success*. Champaign, IL: Human Kinetics, 2015.

Shanley, Ellen, and Colleen Thompson. *Fueling the Teen Machine*. Second edition. Boulder, CO: Bull Publishing Company, 2010.

Steidinger, Joan. *Sisterhood in Sports: How Female Athletes Collaborate and Compete*. Lanham, MD: Rowman & Littlefield Publishers, 2014.

Suen, Anastasia. *A Girl's Guide to Volleyball* (Get in the Game). Mankato, MN: Capstone Publishers, 2012.

USA Volleyball. *Volleyball Systems & Strategies*. Champaign, IL: Human Kinetics, 2009.

Ware, Susan. *Title IX: A Brief History with Documents*. Long Grove, IL: Waveland Press, 2014.

INDEX

A

Association of Volleyball
    Professionals, 10, 48

B

blockers
    how to block, 25–26
    what they do, 16

C

competition, 42–44
coordination, 30

E

eating disorders, 40
endurance, 27–28
equipment, 17

F

Fédération Internationale de
    Volleyball, 10, 48
flexibility, 29

G

goals, 37–39

H

hitters, what they do, 16
Hyman, Flo, 24

I

injuries
    treatment, 34–35
    types of, 32–34

N

nutrition, 39–41

O

Olympics, 9, 10, 20, 24
overtraining, 35–37

P

passing/how to pass, 20–22

R

rally-point scoring, 15

S

serving/how to serve, 18–20

ABOUT THE AUTHORS

Kat Miller grew up in New Jersey and now lives in Brooklyn, New York. She is the author of several books in the Fan Club series.

Claudia B. Manley is a writer who lives in Brooklyn, New York, with her son, partner, and cat.

CREDITS

Sports
other team sports
volleyball